ANCIENT INDIAN EDUCATION

Ancient Indian Education

A Plea for Reintroduction to Arrest the Social Decadence of Modern Times

Nrisinha Prasad Mukhopadhyay

Edited by
Marmar Mukhopadhyay

SHIPRA

Rs. 595; US$ 23.80

ISBN: 978-81-7541-177-7

2014 Impression
(First Published, 2004)

Ancient Indian Education

Published by:
SHIPRA PUBLICATIONS
LG 18-19, Pankaj Central Market,
I.P. Ext., Patparganj, Delhi 110092, India
Ph.: +91 11 22235152/6152, 9650028065
Email: info@shiprapublication.com
www.shiprapublication.com

Dedication

If the author could, he would probably dedicate the book to

Sri Aurobindo

I dedicate it to my Father (the author himself) and to my Mother, who so magnificently nurtured him for more than 75 years

A Presentation

'Ancient Indian Education' generally prompts two kinds of reactions among the educated Indians — cynicism and nostalgia. People educated in 'modern' western knowledge systems gets scared and exclaim, 'Oh no. Not again!' People with background in Indian knowledge systems and access to Sanskrit feel nostalgic. There are few in-between who rationally examine the ancient Indian education system to figure out its relevance and transferability in modern days. This treatise is one of those few.

Contemporary education system services intellectual aspect of life alone, that too superficially. The emphasis on performance in examination and indifference on development of other aspects of human life stands evidence. Superficiality even within this limited focus is further evident from large body of empirical research on levels of cognition vis-à-vis leaning. More serious question is the total absence of educational provision for nurturing the physical, mental and spiritual planes. Despite the flaunting goals of all round development, what education produces is one-dimensional human beings. No wonder, world faces the worst risk of effacing life from our mother earth today than ever before in the history of human civilization. And, the risk is because of the most qualified and informed men and women, and most educated societies and nations.

Education must be revisited with an open mind, away both from nostalgia and cynicism. For, education is the only potent defence against the dangers looming large on human civilization. In this book, author takes a creative look at the ancient Indian education and seeks its relevance today.

A sense of sublime joy, pleasure and privilege dipped with reverence in humility guides the presentation of this scholarly and creative work of Late Sri Nrisinha Prasad Mukhopadhyay, my father, to my fellow readers. He was the founder headmaster of Udang High School in 1933. This piece was authored in 1966-67 out of sheer intellectual excitement; it was his gift to me probably to encourage me to think critically and creatively about the relevance of ancient Indian education system. I was then pursuing my post-graduate studies in education in Calcutta University. More than thirty five years since then; I had a good opportunity to take a fresh look at the manuscript that has now turned yellow with age. I also realized, looking back in my own childhood days, that he practised what he preaches here. It is no theory. I hence decided to share with my fellow colleagues and readers for whatever is its value. I believe, it is pregnant with possibilities of setting a new thought process.

Having seen him from closest quarter, let me share some of the musings from his life that reveals how he practised what he preached, and walked his talk.

Core of ancient educational system is Gurukula where students resided with the Guru and his family that made Guru's life an open book; where they learnt life skills along with pursuit of scholarship.

Despite our own rather 'jealous' economic condition at home, we always had a few students residing with us sharing our food, clothes, reading materials and the scant living space in our village mud-hut. Whosoever (student) showed potential, but at risk (of dropping out), was brought home. My mother's slightest hesitation to accommodate more and deprive her own children was quietened with a profound question, "how do my school children address you?" My mother could not say a word more, her face only brightened up.

For those who stayed with us, obviously his life as well as his entire family was an open book; they shared with pride and joy with other children in the school. They acted as window to his life at home.

He couldn't, obviously have all his students at home. Hence, he made school, the home. When we would get our new shirts and knickers (only one set a year), new clothes will also be bought for school peon and other employees who could not afford; the tiny budget for our clothes was shared with others. 'What's the use of good dresses for the children if the joy is not shared?' Every other teacher in the school, mostly his students, revered him as their teacher and he treated them as his own children.

Ours is a poor community. Despite low fees and fee concessions, many students could not pay even that minimum which was at times less than a rupee. Such outstanding dues were adjusted against his salary and result was declared. Those days, salaries were available once in three months when quarterly government grant was released. But this became a model. Almost every teacher had an account paying fees for poor defaulting students at the end of the year. This we-ness and collectivism successfully broke the boundaries of separation between teachers and students; indeed, it was a family, he was the head.

The school celebrated large number of social, cultural and national events. He and his entire teaching staff were invited to witness the functions. Entire school was literally handed over to senior students. They learnt organizational skills along with several technical skills of paper work, decoration, cooking, preparing pandals, serving, budgeting, purchasing, fund raising, accounting, etc. And, of course, leadership.

Students were least hesitant to 'raid' our house at odd and not-so-odd hours to collect tablecloths, bed sheets, utensils, flower pots or whatever they needed to manage such school programmes. They rarely spared an opportunity to snatch a bite of whatever my mother and sisters would cook. This easy access to our house was an extension of the school. This spread to homes of few more teachers.

My father had a roaring free homoeopathic dispensary; we used to be his compounders during our school days. He learnt homeopathy, as he told me once, to help the village community managing their health — 'how can we teach children who are not healthy?' This holistic concept also comes from

Gurukula concept.

I guess, it was 1964-65, there was skyrocketing of prices of daily consumables including rice which is the staple food of the villagers. There was a hue and cry and near starvation. My father, in consultation with the local leader who was also a medical practisioner decided to give up rice since villagers could not afford. We ate boiled moong, boiled radish and locally available vegetables for nearly three months at a stretch. Once the example was set, villagers took to this new menu; the crisis for rice was over. Thus, he extended the Gurukula concept to cover the entire village community.

He practised Gurukula system by making the entire school, rather the village itself as Gurukula. Yet, he was not a native of Udang. He was brought there in 1933 to head Udang High School. He was given, by one of the villagers, a mud house that we lived till it was washed away in flood in 1978.

No wonder when he retired from life at the age of 90, 30 years after he retired from service, not only educational institutions were closed down, shutters of shops were downed, Central and State establishments like post office and ration (FPS) shops were instantly closed down. Several hundred 'children' wept through the funeral procession. One of the students who received the information late, rushed to the village after the funeral. One who was away in Kolkata and missed, complained to me why didn't we put the news in the newspaper, "are you the only children of Mastermosai!" I could see his honest pains. I had to contain my own sorrow and apologize to him.

His life is a pointer that ancient Indian educational system can be practised meaningfully even today only if we can see beyond ourselves, beyond the narrow boundaries of so called family of blood relations. Today, teachers are much better paid. Thanks to education, their families have also shrunk to smaller size. Imagine if every teacher houses one meritorious poor student at home and provide schooling in his/her school, not only it will change the life of millions of children but also schools become a more honest rendezvous of learning.

Solution is not far, it needs a different way of looking. My purpose of sharing his treasure which only a few of us have access is to see if it inspires one more soul.

Gandhi Jayanti, Marmar Mukhopadhyay
2003
Udang: Howrah

Contents

Contents

Social Decadence of our Times

Every individual in these days – whether the man in the street or of status exulted, people in lots hanging on his lips, feels with a squirm in his heart that there must be something wrong with our society, that affairs are not in the state one wishes or expects them to be in the human order of things. A light seems to have faded, a glory gone - the light, the glory that could guide, make our steps firm. A sense of uncertainty, a vague uneasiness of mind standing under the shadow of a crushing calamity holds us in thrash, - our helplessness-increasing day by day. Nowhere is an inspiration breathed, an utterance soaring or reassuring heard, an example bracing or beckoning met with. We fall short, falter and fumble in every walk of life, haunted constantly by the dissatisfaction that we are not doing the best we could or expected of us. Governments are lax, apathetic, evasive. The administration is corrupt, constrained and compromising. The social morality is at its lowest, and the personal, to all in intents and purposes, non-existent. Groupism and coterie-clicks reign supreme and common people kept in awe of their violent visilations, move like dumb driven cattle under the scourge of their unrestrained ruling rod. No courage to resist, no voice to protest, no faith to do or die. "Is this life - human living in a civilized world? Is life worth living?" is the cry that is forced out of our trembling throats!

Turning to the collective aspect, things appear no more cheering or encouraging. Every nation is distrustful of one another. Pacts, alliances, secret agreements are made with hardly any faith in them, or, with but scant regard to consider obstacle to contrary decision if interest or opportunity points the other way. Military budgets swell from year to year in colossal magnitude and the puny allotment assigned to general welfare and cultural progress, cultivation of human virtues is kept in reserve as first victims for the cold stroke of the pen of policy making hands whenever a cut is felt needed. Violation of convention, mandatory obligations or international laws is the order in the international field. Science pressed into service to invent more and more deadly weapons as a terrorising force and the instrument to bring down quick submission is the preoccupation of the leaders of world politics. The mental spectre of war stalks wide and in dread and confusion we prepare, hastening only its awe-inspiring pace by our very preparedness. And what war! I do not speak the destruction and devastation that every ware more or less carries with it. I mean the cruelties-planned ties premeditated and prosecuted with ruthless thoroughness that are the most conspicuous feature of the present day wars. The scale of mass killing, the shocking sequel held in reserve for the innocent survivors - men in peaceful labour in no way connected with the belligerency rendered deformed, disabled, infected, impotent or begetters only of a progeny as miserable as themselves, nobody knowing how long or for what number of generations the curse is to continue, and land - God's good for nourishing and multiplying made barren parched, robbed of its verdurous smile that soothed, delighted every eye - a picture of dreariness making our head reel. Would it not, one is forced to admit, need a degree of overdosed credulity to believe a posterity- just a few generation remove - a posterity bred and bought up in the atmosphere and under the influence of a line of illustrious forebears who dedicated their all-knowledge, ability resources, nay even life to the amelioration of the lot of their miserable fellow men or raising a fallen brother up, and still sitting under the galaxy of the luminosity of their great doings, engaged in cool deliberations as representatives of advanced states of the time, to spread these abhorrent holocaust. A contrast naturally forces itself upon the mind -- the excellent achievements or the humanitarian departments of United Nations (that but for the conflicting pulls of powers could do much more), in fields of health, social and cultural advancement, education and amelioration of bellicose tension between powers. If nations could join hands in sincerity with genuine goodwill and a little more milk of human kindness what a smiling heaven they could make of this vale of tears. But we build mazeni lines and sigfried walls" instead. Are we then by nature perverse or the delight dearest to our hearts is the thaumaturges one brought by sigh of human misery? No, we are thaumaturges, not believing their ownvit.

But why so? Where is it that the shoe pinches? Causative factors, there are various ends to an unending series, perhaps. The soaring price index with its psychological disquieting effects on the mind of a haunting sense of want, and privation and crippled comfort, the alarmingly growing disparity between food and feeding mouths, the population explosion, the manipulating and speculating profit mongers reducing us to unwilling helpless victims of their profiteering fraud, the diplomatic inconsistency of great powers projecting constantly threats of ruinous wars – all have their shares of dismaying contribution. But the basic cause is elsewhere. We are in throes of an undeclared war, passing through a time of unplanned revolution, thwarted and pushed back, in determined struggle with forces of suppression. Unto the last, men in the lower rungs of the social ladder are bent on riding high and occupying their rightful place by side of honoured ones on the top. They are to wrest away their share of equal enjoyment, social participations in the joys and pleasures of life, corporate so long closed to them and held a taboo for them. Come into their own by the human workship of the Renaissance, weaned away from the crippling inertia and fear of religious domineering by sights of the holiest citadels of after-life glory and happiness battered down by doctrinaring quarrels, and sectarian preachings of the Reformation, roused to ardourn of action by the inspiring philosophy, new dreams of a dignified social order and actual achievements of the French revolution, disciplined and made more confident through experiences of political movements of recent times, they are not to give in. But the powers that be, the ousters of forgotten days, the usurpers of remote history, the exploiters of our time are as adamant and will not cede an inch of ground. They cannot be without having a class lower down - their hated ragamuffins or labelled socially, perhaps with a sprinkling of pity, 'the hewers of wood and drawers of water' to stand in wait to cater for their needed comfort or embellished luxury, and serve for the menial offices too low for their high life ways, and the class must be perpetuated. The lesson of history is lost on them. Humanity has no appeal to them. The dictates of time they seek to circumvent in the case of their confidence in power. People are divided and polarised. Countries are convulsed and the foolish tussle goes on, while the true course would be to resolve the crisis with as little bitterness and adhorent excesses on either side in the interest of national solidarity and individual amity, we fan the fire, each side trying by means, fair or foul, to work the dun-doing of the other. The obstinacy of power break never bends. Unthinkable excesses, unashamed misdoings, ruinous strategies are invited into the scene portending permanent disruption and creation of dangerous pockets like cankers eating into the vitals of national life. "Mankind is incorrigible", cried in despair well-meaning acute H.G.Wells. But that is too pessimistic. Let us educate ourselves better.

Ancient Indian Education: Arresting Force

In these contexts, it is our business to consider the possibilities of Ancient Indian Education as a retarding, if not reclaiming, force to arrest the decadence. 'Ancient Indian Education-el' I hear the buzz and bursts of surprised voices with ill-concealed annoyance. The education of men with primitive ideas, habits and mental make up! What have we in common with them - men of debated manners and shadowy history to profit thereby - with science, sociology, experiments and enlightenments of these days at our service. Is our system, the western fashion and of worldwide acceptance, inadequate or incompetent? Pray, let them alone - the slumbering dead in their peaceful vaults lying for scores of centuries. Or if the old times - the good old times be the fancy why pass over the claims of the Buddhist, the Moslem, the Christian systems with so many similar features and modes of imparting equal rivals in reputation and quite as great? Yes, no question of bypassing, nor of any fancy. It is need dictating. Those systems are quite good as far as they go, but tied down each to its own philosophy and goal of life, their several religions impose on them. Philosophies cripple, life expands and soars, challenging even the vaults of heaven. Life is greater than all philosophies taken together. We want a system for life itself- that stupendous fact and surpassing mystery of creation. Ancient Indian Education meets our need admirably. 'But does it too not impose and restrain as every system is bound to?' A question again! No, it does not, for it is in the elements of life's being the stuff and substance with diffused urge and innate proneness awaiting concentration, integration and manifestation. What we should strive towards is a free, full, pervasive education stimulating all that is best in us to a rounded-flowering in the colour and splendour of life's own glory. Here the Ancient Indian system is unique.

To my mind, the western system, as we have it today with its principle of growth re-innovation and flexibility to adapt itself constantly to the demands of an emerging society, is in most ways an ideal one. But it has a grave lack - the gravest perhaps when put on the background of insistent demand of our present day society and chaos of world conditions. I mean the lack of the ideal, the goal to strive after - the finished product answering to immediate need. We have to face and bring under control the malaise we now suffer from. The Western system leaves the goal an open question, or at best tries for all-round competence with scarcely any emphasis on deeper questions of life, the truth of creation and existence, a competence throwing very superficial lights on a worthy living and a true fulfillment. It confines its business to putting into the taught a body of knowledge well thought-out and carefully selected, no doubt, to enjoy life and deal with the world in the way most advantageous here to his purpose, so it falls short. The possession is well-arranged equipment for life, not for life itself if we feel no need or urge that way.

Brahmacharyashram

But the Ancient Indian Education is an all-out coordinated endeavour directed to the one aim of knowing the truth of life and fashioning it in accord. And what is that truth? The greatest and perfect one ever reached by devotion, discipline and dire dedication of man. The educational phase, first of the four phases, comprising the *Varnashram* order, conceived in the light of a perfected whole is designated *Brahmacharyashram*. The word ordinarily means abstention from all matters pertaining to sex, but literally and derivatively means a life in Brahma (God), with the mode of living activities in harmony with His ways. The preceptors spared no pains to hold the disciple fast to the way, tuned in inspiration and action to that rare high aim and rare ideal.

Brahma - a term coined and contributed to the philosophy of God by the Indian mind, in virtue of its peculiar appeal and particular approach and apprehension of the Supreme Being, is the same as God of the popular notion - both the imanent and transcendental aspects included, but with the difference that here the whole emphasis is laid on the aspect of its vastness. The word literally means the big one, but the bigness here is beyond all imagination, passes comprehension with limits we never know of extent, depth and height. It contains the whole of cosmic universe and yet has room enough to contain many more. In fact, nothing can be conceived that can remain outside the bounds of Brahma. Not biggers alone, it is the only stuff of the material creation - all appearances in the multiplicity of name and form are but figments being at bottom and in ultimate analysis merely Brahma stuff. The truth has been reached by our Rishis (vedic seers) by direct apprehension in deepest contemplation called *'samadhi'* and taught through ages including our own time by our saints and savants, mystics and masihas, prophets and preachers and has gone down as an inalienable part in the concept of Indian life. The glory, splendour and the stupendousness of the vision of the truth is unmatched in the range of human experience, and only the mind carried to supramental levels is capable of the vision in moments of perfect concentration or meditation. The mind stilled, sunk into the depths of being, senses withdrawn and completely detached from its in and outgoing activities, the consciousness of individuality almost evaporated even the weight of physical body quite melted away. There appearing in the diffused, very vague sense of existence a calm, ineffable feeling of delight pouring in with a pervading light, soft, soothing but, at the same time, refulgently glorious and brought a condition anon replaced by an overwhelming floods of light engrossing all and effacing all material distinctions immersed in the light, the meditator is brought face to face with the inmost truth and ultimate stuff of the material creation. The appearances are mere ripples on the breast of the calm and constant sea bubbles on water surface. The sea of light is Brahma - putting forth and absorbing in its essence in its vastness existences separated while the state of mind still lasted and varied that we call creation. The Rishi, filled to the full in the delight of being and released from the narrow bonds of separative existence, cries out in thrilled exultation in symbols and semblances - for Brahma is indescribable and beyond imposition of form – I have known the Great one haloed in the glorious colour of the sun and beyond approaches of all darkening shadows. In that knowledge is the release from the bondage of the existence of narrow individuality in the vastness of being as God's. The appeal and impression of this vastness, the desire to expand life in mission with the rare ideal is so great in Indian mind irrespective of personal status, occupation and living pattern as to be almost a national trait with the Indians. And who would challenge this breath of outlook and this universal sympathy of kindredship with everything in creation can be the only panacea for the evils that our countries and our societies now suffer from. Ancient Indian education made it its one business to incu lcate this ultimate truth and discipline, inspiration and action of the disciples in tune with this unique ideal life in Brahma. The preceptors as teachers in deep reverence and sincere adorationas colleague, disciples or successors to carry forward the tradition as they proved themselves more capable of this vision and competent enough to put it into the possession of their pupils. They would spare no pains to carry this charge to this singular elevation. This education is, therefore, the desideratum of fulfillment of individual life and prosperity of our society at large in these times.

Two very intricate problems - interesting and edifying, at the same time here, shoot up demanding resolution. If this be the truth, what of this world - so solid, so matured, so potent in its unseen but irresistible power to hold us down to its own ways, despite all our contrary wishes and desires - the world with its mad rush of events, its noise and hustle and breathless hurry, its soaring and shattering impacts on events or courses of our life, its lights of triumphant advance, its nights of undoing defeats, its brave advance and grave impasse - what are these and what of these? Again, what of our individual life - our so loved and so fondly fed delighting and deluging us at every step with the in-pouring of satisfied self-glory at every successful self-assertion with the flooding relish satisfaction coming through competent self-assertion - its will to power, to possession and position. This hungry hunt after enjoyment and thrills, this facing of odds for success, their crafts and crooks to avoid failures, the race to overtake, the dark designs to over-reach this jealousy, this vying, these sleep-killing dreamings and designings - what all these come to - the congeries of hunt and excitement, we call life, What remains, in point of fact, for us to do? A great deal, indeed the greatest deal.

Perhaps, if we understand the basic objectives - to make of us God, rising to his status, and in the consciousness of freedom from narrow individuality, to work in vast sweeps as his co-worker for the fulfillment of his purpose in creation. This is not to spurt down, as most of us wrongly think, all enjoyments and delights of life, and enter the dreary world of loin cloth, somber-face, fasting and self-chasting and seeding life to wearisome decay. For otherwise, to love God and emulate His doing is to take to the world with more zest, with more relish as love is then all embracing and fully free begetting a self-satisfaction and self-delight, this life of narrow interest and demanding self-seeking can never know. We are now turned into God's gardener entrusted with this field of life of infinite possibilities for a bumper to bless the world with its harvest. But beware of the responsibility. If the ordinary burden of material living be so crushing, how infinitely heavier is the responsibility you have called upon yourself - the extraordinary responsibility of carrying a God in you with the duty of keeping his glory unsullied and his power not impinged upon.

A very illuminating example is furnished by the life of Sri Aurobindo, a seer of our own time, and of world-wide renown as a divine man; a famous Cambridge scholar, and with a strange irony of fate, sent to England at the age of seven to keep him out of contact with Indian culture and way of life. When in jail, as a political prisoner, he had 'Basudev Darshan' that is, he saw with his material vision the indwelling God in every separate form of created life - in man, in cattle grazing, in trunks, branches, even leaves of trees, in every man in the assembled course of trial. The trying magistrate, lawyers for and against him - all and everything about – are symbols inspiring Godhead. He used to advise his lawyer on the day before the case was to come up for hearing. The lawyer as usual came, but he refrained from any advising and told him to do what he thought best. How could he, when all are God, without sinning against God by discriminating and seeking selfish interest? Sri Aurobindo took forty years since Darshan (his vision) to realise his vision. Work there is in plenty and of the gravest moment. An unrelenting and unending devotion to God in every inch of the being. Do not pine but aspire on. With the Promethean fire lodged in us, how can we laze, lark in follies and frivolities leaving this tremendous gift unintended? The concern with us is, as Plato has said, to 'light the shadow of God! Let us address ourselves, shedding off all weakness and lures of ephemeral pleasures, to this task of supreme attainment.'

I perceive the surprise and bewilderment I throw my modern readers into with their outlook, ambition, and standard of values of these times. It is perhaps the same surprise or more, Columbus, and Larde of adventurer after him, landing at various points of America, felt as they came upon vast fields of gold and silver lying virgin all over the countries. Surprise, indeed but only superficial, the reason being the Europeans know and the Barbarian natives knew not the value and use of the precious metals. Very similar is the case here also - our ancestors knew and we know not the value and glory of this life. To make the point clear we will be well advised to make some gleanings in the field of our Yajnas - so popular and considered so potent in achieving purposes in the Vedic times.

Yajnas
Reaching out to God Like Stature

Broadly speaking, the Vedic Yajna was a ritualistic-cum-propitiatory workshop on lines prescribed by the Vedas to realise the end the performer might have in view, somewhat like the wishfilling tree of mythology. It is infallible in its effect, so much that it is kept alive as a part of the ceremony of our image worship of these days. The nuptial and the thread wearing rites of the Brahmins are fully patterned on the Yajna model. Even actual Yajna in perfect congruence with Vedic programme, though rare, is not abandoned in our days. The practice survives, the significance is forgotten and lost. We go repeating the sound of valet's duties without ever turning to the Knight of the show. Yajnas were of varieties -

big and small, daily, seasonal, occasional and incidental to the purpose of the performers. In fact, the Yajna was the only ceremonial rite obtaining currency in Vedic India and the core business everywhere was to immolate something - usually wood soaked in butter oil – into the holy fire and burning it down. Every ceremony, however, having features peculiar to itself - the big ones like Aswamedha were in scale and grandeur elaborate ritualistic observances, and fabulously extravagant expenditure in gift making, charity and entertainments - animal killings exceeded the highest feats of imagination. The yajna was supposed to be capable of altering the trend of material events and the character of these courses in favour of the objective the performer seeks.

It is on these scores - the uninspiring, crude, commonplace, repugnent features, as attributed with crafty gainful hooks – that the yajna practice along with the 'samheta' and Brahman parts of the Veda countenancing, stimulating and elaborating it, has come in for an unmerited condemnation in the hands of Western Vedic scholars, and thus Indian followers who messed wholly their real and deep lying significance. Sri Aurobindo - a seer and a considerable linguist conversant with mystiques of words has dispelled the mist and taken us to the heart of things. And what a heart of gold is there, lying neglected because of our ignorance and unimaginative thought and ways carved on materialistic, mental approach of our time. The yajna business is, in the main symbolic, but not altogether divorced from their material features,.kept associated in a complementary relation to hughten impression and carry-home significance. Considered, in this light, all are found to be in place, advancing meaning and ensuring effect. The treatment of the western scholars is *prima facie* and from angles of wordly valuation. But scholarship without imagination, broach and almost of a lynical kind is out of place here. It fails to reach the world of thought combination of which yajna is the material projection. The performance is stripped of its spirit and is therefore, dead matter. The spiritual vision going as reaction hand in hand with material performance gives rife to the thing, and yajna reaches it full status when we take things together.

All yajna are, we may say, based on the maxim - first deserve, then desire – and the secret of its infallibility must be sought then. Here, we divinise life through vows, practices and through recasting of thought trends in reference to Brahma concept, that is, to put the thing more concretely, fashion a life in thought and behaviour, if he is to assume a personal form in flesh and blood. In other ways, yajna is a subtle and certain process - tried, tested and applied by our Brahma's (priests) to concentrate and draw forth the divine substance in us mixed up, bedimmed, lying lulled and vitiated in association with gross elements of the body and improper uses under influence of worldly lures. Yajna burns it pure out of its dross and makes us Godman.

To turn now to the symbolic aspect, with the caution already given. The chief business in the performance is to pour libation - choice things such as butter oil, holy leaves and flowers, perfumes – into fire to be burnt down. The first is the insatiable urge of the soul to come into the perfection of divine life, and the burning is the amiculation of gross possessions and the most powerful attachment to them. The animal killing is the sacrifice of the animalities in us. The gift making is belittling the worth of possession and discipline in non-attachment for the benefit and prosperity of creation. The yajna performance must be a munificent giver says the Vedas, for the great achievement is not for all, but only for a chosen few. Yajna is a minutely planned, very carefully coordinated and properly and fully limbed performance to help the blessed ones to rise to the status of God. It is in the nature of man to grow. We grow, our smaller self is constantly outreached by our bigger self and finality is not reached till we attain God-like stature, being master of nature and creation. But not human efforts alone, but the grace of divine must work propitiously to bring about the elevation. Now, the grace is there in abundance and constant pouring. The mind is also striving. But the gap is unfilled - the grace not finding correct vessel, the striving falling short of its exact mark. Yajna bridges the gulf, drawing down grace, on the one hand disciplining the performer, on the other. Here, fire is god - God-embodiment of all gods and the most powerful agent to enlist their grace. The actions, strictly ordered performed in a correct manner, elaborate ritualism, accompanied with the rhythmic chantings of Vedic formulas and hymns, the fire hissing and leaping, investing all around in its golden glow, and, above all the, Om sound, – the embodiment of the Being in the sound element of creation - rising incessantly and in all directions, filling and making the whole atmosphere vibrant with it; the performer, invariably always of high social status sitting meek and salient, in prayerful lowliness washed of all vanities of power and possession only meditating the state he is coming into, a scene solemn and extraordinary is presented expectant of a great birth that is hardly to be disbelieved. Yes, there is a birth - tremendous passing ordinary comprehension. A Godman, the divine being in the frail vessel of human form, come into being. The tenement of clay is turned into a dwelling of God - all refulgent with the vast glory and passing brilliance of Godness with the existence dedicated to the good of creation alone. Yajna is the sure and secure vehicle, contrived by our Rishis to take us Godward till the indwelling God in man, the God of creation, and God, the Lord of creation are condensed into one human form, free in love, power and knowledge, treating mortal as the soil of earth. Detachment, renunciation, self-discipline and self-purging to God's perfection are instruments of the process.

Renunciation

It is by renunciation alone that the supreme state of transcendental immortality is reached, say the Vedas and it is repeated incessantly by Vivekananda. A famous vedantist of our time has it - our life all through is a grand process of Yajna. Rabindranath, the divine poet in an inspiration of transcendantal lyric, thus, bursts forth in music - 'I care not if this my frail narrow vessel of human mind is broken down to pieces, for I am sure your grace will make it large and fill it to the brim with divine nectar'. In reality, the true business of our life is to break through our narrow worldliness and make it vast in the vastness of God. Sri Aurobindo, commenting on the topic, says – 'By right sacrifice .... man can achieve all things.

He shall conquer his perfection; Nature shall come to him as a willing and longing pride; he shall become her seer and rule her as her king.' The sum and substance of all these is that yajna gives our mind a new turn far removed from worldliness but perfectly close to the world to re-mark our life with a new approach to its affairs with a view to giving birth to a new world worthy of human living. Needless to add, Yajna was not for all, nor did all participate in the performance. But the high objective, the faith and discipline, the enthusiasm attached to it inspired and influenced all lives, so that it became a living reality to guide and control the Indian way of life with the strongest force. Ancient Indian Education breathed with this inspiration, practiced in an atmosphere permeated and interspersed with ideals, visions of life and examples of self-discipline unmatched, imparted, more or less, by the very nature of the show, cannot but have for its finished product men with whom, detachment, renunciation and utter self-sacrifice for the well-being of mankind and creation are as natural and habitual as the breath of our nostrils. It is the adequate and apposite education that can really deal satisfactorily with problems confronting us in our age.

By a strange irony of fate, our lives are cast in a world of things and people behaving more wonderfully than perhaps those Alice came across in her Wonderland everyday, and from every country we have solemn declarations bubbling with sympathy for the misery of people and amelioration of their lot, that, if translated into action could deluge the world with milk and honey in a few hours. But misery is on the increase on both the physical and the mental side of man. The small but usual philanthropy residing in economic corruption and political disruption. The common man, if not in the service of a party, has no prospect of a livelihood. In the midst of plethora, not a very rare phenomenon in these days, thanks to the boom of black money men, far out-numerbing those fortunate harmful ones, are starved to skeleton, the funny parade of personal pride and foolish waste in display of affluent life, going on by the side, heedlessly, heart busy with its silly noise of overflowing plenty, the mockery of fellow sympathy shedding off its false guise. Here, we postulate a race of man whose philanthropy is no social disguise for name and fame, but attribute of being, pouring in God's plenty to resuscitate and prosper creation on, it never before knew. 'They kingdom come' has been the dream cry on every lip of man in one language or another since the dawn of creation, but we have run headlong the opposite till the present ruinous state is reached. The throne must be brought down and placed in a surrounding compatible with its high heavenly glory. But the high destiny must be attained through the agency of human instruments unless we rest on our faith in miracles - certainly not a flattering comment on the high possibilities claimed for man. Men such as these only can aspire to undertake the high task, save the world and fulfill the noble purpose of god in creation.

The topic was introduced to explain the rather unfamiliar aim of education in ancient Indian life, running strangely counter to all acknowledged of a successful career according to - standards of our time, thus putting my finger on a rare and exceptional trait of Indian life. I have perhaps lingered also a little long on it, but of purpose. Renunciation and detachment are in the blood of our people, not to say the most powerful tradition to dominate and determine the course of our life, but unfortunately a truth we are almost forgetting. The *Ramayana* and the *Mahabharata* are still the cradle of our childhood, Buddha, the founder of a rival faith received a place in the Hindu Pantheon as a God incarnate.

Ashok, the Great, lived a saintly life of sacrifice and service only for the good of his subjects. This missionary zeal for peace and friendliness among people, his devoted nursing of the living world from the meanest to the mightiest have become the subject of universal praise and admiration of all history. Conqueror Samudra Gupta, the *Alexander* of India, is recorded to have performed Aswamedha. Harsha surnamed Shiladityoera (a sun among men of high conduct) emptied his royal treasury of its accumulations of five years, giving in charity to worthy persons, and in his famous congregation at Prayag, giving in charity his royal robe, he wore at the end. Sri Aurobindo declining the enamoured I.C.S. and beginning career as personal secretary to the Gaikward of Baroda, changing the high post for a professorship, and then leaving these to be the editor of a national paper, his material prospects and monetary gains dwindling all the while in the series of succession, and going to jail for his bold national demands as a political leader, and finally passing into the seclusion of a contemplative life for the good of the world in dire privation is a rare example of a renunciated life in our days.

Gandhiji: A Renunciate

Some room must be found here for a mention - a special and stressed mention, I should say, of Gandhiji, though not one in the orthodox tradition of spiritual masters of religious luminaries on Indian life. Gandhiji, the most famous son of recent India, a world figure of massive influence, a subject of endless criticism and comment, kind and unkind, favourable or adverse, who chose politics for his sphere of action, and threw asunder the established order of state craft of the world by his unorthodox ways of approach to it, basing practical politics on what he thought to be a duty to God and mankind at large. He entered politics not for gain or fame nor even for power to rule but simply to rescue politics from its unworthy motivations and unscrupulous practices. He is a saint in politics. Diplomacy is a word not to be found in his dictionary. All is open and outspoken with him. The adversary is put before hand into the knowledge of his line of attack; the shape of his strategy to be forwarded and prepared for resistance, for him adversary is no enemy, but a person or party with misguided zeal bent on perpetuating a human wrong or some debasing untruth. He was the first to break through the political doctrine of Kautilya and Machiavelli and base it on the *Geeta* where the voice of God is speaking.

With him the distinction between affairs temporal and spiritual did not prevail, secularism and theocracy are senseless demarcations, artificial, injurious, an affront to God's impartial and equal dispensation. He condemned the silly wisdom of keeping Caesar's and Pant's dues apart and calculating them on two kinds of Arithmetic. All dues of man are to Pant - the world of man's dealing, is a Vatican of God. His belief is inflexibility anchored on the clean and plain logic, it seems - how can man with but one life, one mind and one soul – hence, one angle of vision accede to different standards of conduct without hypocricy or concession to untruth? He would countenance no unjust restraint on man's freedom of thought, action and equality of social rights, as they are things leading astray from his path of God, casteism, a foolish social distinction made on the accident of birth, limiting the equality of man as ordained by impartiality, living together in heaven is a hateful stain on generosity of man and in the social body, a curse crippling social solidarity, stimulating fissiparous tendencies in the social structure. Untouchability is to him a sin against God – sacrilegious irreverence to the shrine that he has chosen to dwell in on earth. Wherever he went, he made his stay in the scavengers' settlement, an area considered unclean and would take food touched by them. He took the most frugal and simple meals respecting the claims of other members of the society to a justified share, wore a piece of loin cloth because his countrymen were ill-clad. His political movements, nearly always a one man's show, as it must be, to which the whole native, with diverse state-of-art leaders of different castes, culture and community, having sharp divisions as to the potential goal to be fought for, responded like one man, which, at least in one case, according to competent observers, came within an inch of success reared into being in the cradle of his God-guided mind and shaped for action in the cleanest consume, undefected by motives of victory on advantage of fighting operations. And what unequal fights they were - a frail, inscrutable man of the strongest ways opposing with his spiritual personality only, the British rule, the mightiest imperialism of the world, with endless military and material resources deployed to the full in ruthless aggressiveness, and our and his hand remained clean all through the face of the gravest presentation, his soldiry submitting to cruel torture and to provoking ill-treatment, suffering with noblest human dignity, set an example of moral fighting unthought of before in any phase of history. His method of operation was non-cooperation nonviolent – discreation from acts morally wrong and unjust without physical violence and with minds full of pity and love like a father's to a prodigal son. His contribution in the independence of India is and will ever remain a matter of controversy. But that he, with his acute practical genius and the guidings of India's spiritual traditions, fashioned a powerful weapon for effective use, wherever wronged humanity suffers, is beyond all controversy.

The half naked father standing in a solitary nook of history without trumpet and arms without noisy propagandist following sheds on the course of events affecting human destiny and holding God in bondage a lustre that will never fail to inspire men fighting for a just social order in which generosity of human goes linked with the unbounded mercy of God. To him, the lame spirituality, sitting in secluded place away from the misery of deprived of contemplation and well-wishing humans, is not enough. It must be carried afield, made militant, brought to grips with conditions granting the evils base of life. Man's social living and political dealing must be changed to banish them for good from the world we have to live in. His renunciation to the uttermost limits of his possession – may be surprising or outwitting to even pious minds piously inclined that way. He declared truth is God and reflected his faith in it in the most brilliant and unscrupulous way on all he did and dictated. He is faithful to God as any saintly soul could be. His detachment, another cardinal condition, according to Indian standards of spiritual living, doubted and, on occasions, seriously questioned, must be correct and satisfying to him from his own angle of vision, and who can challenge the detachment of a man who standing under the shadow of very real threats to his life, a threat that in no distant time materialised, kept unflinchingly to his chosen path of action as an aricle of faith and a commandment of God, and as the sole meaning of life lived. Gandhiji is not outside, but in the full stream of India's spiritual tradition, with a greater and graver dimension so long lacking, boldly added to it.

The tradition runs on still unabated, never undervalued, not merely in the life of numerous saints and sages, religious masters flourishing through ages and in all parts of the country, but has, to this day, the greatest hold on the minds of our people and is the strongest drive to our aspiration. India is perhaps the singular country under the sun where a spiritual worthy, nearly naked, with unkempt hair and a shabby blank wrap, is given as high an ovation as the state president or premier or any crowned head can hardly expect. Renunciation and dedication to the good of creation are still with us a most dominant inspiring force as nothing else is. Here is a Naoh's are ladden with the possibilities of all prosperous future germination, after the depletion of the deluge of our present destructive civilization, our immortal patrimony to lend to the bankrupt world of the nearing future. Let us not fritter it away, borne on the drift of the current self-centred living and enjoyment.

Student: The Disciple

It is said - India has changed much under the impact of the industrial civilization of the West. Perhaps so, if we confirm our observation to the surface only. But India has come in contact with many alien cultures and people before. Much we have taken in, much we have given up always picking the best flowers rejecting the defective ones of the lots to thread them into a perfect garland of divine weaving in our native fashion. The fact is - we cannot go round or draw ourselves off from the fascination of beauty and power of eternal India – sitting silent, changeless amidst rushing changes, self-absorbed in the glory of her renunciation and non-possession, contemplating only the good of man and the universe. The deathless India in our hearts growing, expanding and perfecting itself is still always the guide, discipline and the goal of our aspiration, guiding, restraining and inspiring in our thought and conduct; and, be it known for certain, that any new bargain can only impoverish, never bring any grist.

With these prior preparations and mental adjustments - for a preparation and adjustment is needed to apprehend fully a life so simple on the surface, so profound in depth in its multicoloured, many pronged significance, let us be ready for a sally of a day's sojourn to keep the company of a Vedic time disciple as he presses through his daily round of duties staying at this preceptorial home - it was a 'must' with the disciples during the period of their education. Away from the bargaining noise of the market place of cities and towns, away from the calculating, constricting, narrowing forces of the home life atmosphere, the preceptorial seats situated in calmly plains abutting on spreading deep forests -these abounded in the country in those days of sparse population, and usually with a holy river or a cool streamlet of limped water rolling by, breathed a calm, composure and other worldliness that at once lulls down the agitating – interest seeking and selfish longings of worldly inducement and makes us feel big of heart. His day began before the first glows of dawn were yet to tinge the sky - an hour of calm never yielded by any other time of the day. The birds are awake, but not carolling, the towering ancestral trees wrapped in transparent darkness interspersed with faint peeps of light looking like sages in meditation, the ferocious denizens in the bowels of the forest not yet rounded to activity - it is the hour when with a dip in the love and mercy of her creator, nature revitalises the world for its approaching ordeal of the day. He rises, says his short prayer for the blessing of the day for himself and the creation, and goes out to his bath. The bath is ceremonial as much as it is material. The merits of all holy rivers are involved into his water the whole ablution is accompanied with intoning of Vedic lines and singing of hymns. This done, he goes next to the forest to collect chips of wood for 'homa' a daily duty next after bath, never to be traversed. The business is no tiring one, but rather intensifies the mental pity and serenity by its calm breeze and shadowy mystery of the forest depths. He comes back not merely refreshed but differently inspired for his day's duties ahead. He performs the 'Homa', ceremonially a yajna, in memature and done in the same spirit - his first sacrifice into fire of the day for his spiritual advance and the good of creation and the world. The fire pits, severally assigned to every participant, extend in rows the fire burning and liberations consumed - regaling the air with fragrance far around present a scene charged with divine inspiration. After 'Homa' they all rise facing east to the rising sun, chant Vedic prayers and hymns in fullthroated emotional effusion and the voice vibrant with that primodial sound 'Om' that is God's very self. At once it washes off his individual limitations, plunging them into the vastness and benign feeling, that is God. It is indeed a sight for gods to see, and it holds the atmosphere resounded long with a living holiness of influence, we can hardly imagine, far less feel. Then they go to greet their guru and are told off to the several duties of the day for his household.

The preceptor, we must be reminded is also a big householder with family, the disciples, hosts, guests, visitors and casual seekers of hospitality. The household duties are, therefore, not neglected here or minimised in importance. Rather, being a man of knowledge and of high spiritual experience and attainments, the preceptor unfolds a family life true to the kindred points of heaven and home, or proper and generous hospitability a spotless way of living life and the household ideals zealously guarded by high traditions of family life duties on Indian thinking furnishing models to disciples who are soon to be householders on their own account, at the conclusion of their period of residential education. Rabindranath gives in his poetic way the ideal to be followed. The domesticity is to be pursued always with the presence of Brahma in the mind. The friendless, the ailing, the distressed should find a true home here with free admission into its shelter, succour and attention. A valedictory address on the eve of a disciple's leaving his preceptorial shelter runs thus - Never wander away from truth, from the well being of man and society and creation, from the Vedas, and the injunctions of religion. Do only what is approved and accepted by society.

Avoid all that is blamed or thought to detract from the good of it. Parents, guests and those coming to you on visit or business should be looked upon as God. Give with grace and fear, lest your manners hurt the feeling of the recipient. Give not in neglect or disrespectful ways. Be your life a service to creation. Thus, each disciple setting up a household became a centre of uplifting force for the neighbourhood - its friend and philosopher and the other way, the depository of the people's love and regard.

In the afternoon, as the day grows mellow, the sun rays soft and cajoling, the disciples broke up into conclaves and gathered round the preceptor or advanced students for a most intimate and free interchange of thoughts to clear difficult points on the subjects of their study or for deeper penetration. In the evening, the morning programme was more or less repeated. They retired rather early after a frugal and wholesome supper for recapitulation of the old and attempts at the new studies, contemplation and sleep. The entire business is so simple, that to dignify the process with the name of a system is straining a point. It was a natural system or rather nature's system. But who would challenge that, it still remains the high watermark of pedagogy. The more energetic and curious students supplemented their knowledge by attendance at yagna centres, where debates, discussion, dissertations among the assembled worthies were a regular feature associated with the yagna arrangements. They also appeared at the congregations of outstanding spiritual luminaries who, from time to time, met at places of holy fame to exchange mutual thoughts and experiences to bring new light or clear their own doubts and where rare bits of knowledge of the highest order were picked up. In fact, enlargement and enrichment of the mind with daily studies was a life-time vow with every disciple and 'light, more light' was the most pious, predominant and pervading cry of his being, for here was liberation from the bondages of existence and rise to higher and still higher existence. Manu gives an elaborate code of discipline for the disciples during tutelege - all of sterling value, embodying the highest wisdom of life, no doubt, reflecting the injunctions and practices of the Vedic times - one that may still be a citation one, for instance: cleanse body with earth and water, but know for certain to be clean in matters of money dealings is the highest of all cleanliness. But we wanted to present the totality of the pattern and need not go into the detail.

Modern Life Habits
The Contrast

While presenting this outline one is irresistibly drawn to a contrast by placing by the side the picture of the life habits in our modern times. Is not this a life ' only dressed for show' - all on the surface without aim, without restraint, without ideals to guide our steps, with hectic hurry, with noising in the excitement of the moment from thrusts of business and problems of life and work insisting. With an apology of a bath, with a hasty meal somehow we jump out, run with breakneck speed to be in time - we can rarely be punctual, at the post of our duty, and spend the bright brave hours of the day in the unrelieved dissembling of our personality - false friendliness, false well-wishing, false show of interest in the benefit of others for a pose of our high-minded generosity - the eye like a vulture's, fixed on our personal gain and advancement - without sincerity, without emotional ardour, without even a ray coming of a properly lived human life. We return towards the fag end of the day spent up, bored, glum from the effects on the mind of the false performances carried through the long hours till from daily repetitions truth and falsehood loose colours and become all gray, - and gray, is the colour of our life and the world of our movement. The evenings are crowded and stretched far into the night spent in clubs, bars, cinema houses, friendly visits or may be at respectable conferences of the elite, or parties or functions arranged. With a disquieted restless sleep, induced by tranquillizers, we rise late, unrefreshed, unrecouped - a heavy listless mind. This is, however, our time to enjoy, - to taste the delight of 'Homa', sweet home' and warmth of social intimacy, with a cup of steaming tea before us with the day's news paper and we chat with wife, our children, hear fondly their complaints, receive friends, visitors and guests with, however, the ugly face of the day's duties ahead looming before our eyes to disturb the somehow snatched peace. Children bred in the atmosphere absorbing the influence of the example and knowing full well to be called upon soon enough to step into these shoes - what kind of discipline, seriousness of life, of value of character can you expect? We are burning the candle at both ends - a generation throwing the precious energy of human life to waste, a posterity growing up in a vacuum, a prey to the propensities of nature. What but utterly benighted listing can be in store for us? Two questions here rear up their heads and must be answered. Is not this, the life of a small section of society? Yes, but is not that society, the 'Babus' centre of gravity of the ambition of the largest mass below the level? The second and most difficult one for adequate answer is - what is there for an alternative? We want to live and must live, but certainly, more honourably and in our Indian way - like Vidyasagar or many a worthy men of our own time, or as our ancestors lived, in poverty but with true dignity, can't we? I humbly submit with more erectness, infusing more strength into our backbones roll back the trend of time by manful protest of attitude.

Two anecdotes from two very ordinary lives I put forward not in support, but simply for consideration or as an alternative way of my point. The first is of a railway porter. A gentleman detraining quite late at Agra Station on an inclement night with luggages got into a fix as to how to get to his destination. The porter offered to carry the luggage on eight annas, but the quantity being too heavy for one man proposed to call in another, but warned he would take advantage of the inclemancy and might demand five to six rupees. Under pressure of situation his services, however, were purchased for five and fifty. But this porter took only eight annas. Questioned why he too did not take advantage of the inclemency? He said that he was doing the work by way of spiritual discipline under the bidding of his religious master and was not to earn more than the cost of his daily living. The eight annas were just what he needed that day. The other story relates to a cobbler by the roadside. A gentleman came for a mending of his shoes, and being pleased with the cheap offer of four annas, concluded the bargain, with doubts, however, the work might be negligent and watched on keenly. The work was done carefully and perhaps with more than ordinary conscience. For he mended carefully and examined the whole shoe for any other weaker parts. Remuneration paid, the cobbler bagged his tackles with haste and rose up. It was about the time of sunset and not the time to leave work. Impelled by curiosity, the gentleman followed him at a distance, and when the man came up from his bath in the Ganges, pressed him for an explanation of his riddling conduct. The answer extorted was that his was a life of religious austerities under guidance of a master who had restricted his daily earning to two rupees for himself and his family. The hour was for his contemplating and daily religious practices, but he still lacked four annas, hence the hurry, and all that he noticed? What is particularly uncommon about them, - it will be argued. They are men in the lower station of life and of humble birth and have nothing of the ambition goading us. Is not this religious cloak a protection a badge of self-exultation against the cold behaviour of social indifference doled out to them?

Nay! what man there is in normal psychology and in normal deal of life to brush away an honest and rightful gain unless he has a different standard of evaluation. They know more than we are prepared to credit them with. They have come into that possession, beside which the world's gifts pale into insignificance -God's way and the life of glory in them.

'A dazzling *chir-ma-rd*' I hear the nestor voice of ill-concealed satire of my friend, the intellectual, as the word is chewed down his lips in disbelief and disapprobation punctuated with rhythmic nod of his learned head boiling with Science, Sociology, Psychology and emporiums of modern knowledge, constantly reinforced by gains of foragings in new fields of research and experiment. I perceive the ripplings and twisting of his grave face with a touch of pity – an enlightened pity to be sure, that so much labour and attention should be bestowed on so absurd a matter. He goes on. 'A Utopia, after all, - no doubt of clever design and careful finish but - the pity of it will not hold water. Life is no airy bloom, but a growth on a material plant with roots fixed on the hard ground providing sap and nourishment'. 'Yes, yes, who denies it? We are all nursed on the cosy and sustaining breast of the ever-loving mother earth. But what about the fragrance - on the bed of petalic beauty, and unmixed of the smell of any dirt the soil may contain. I conceive life in terms of fragrance not rejecting but sublimating material acquisitions an art life is capable of. I hear now the less robust voice of the distracted common man, oscillating between enthusiasm and suspicion. It were good if things could be so moulded. But where to find the preceptors of that high ideal of life and that powerful personality to level down all obstacles in the way and carry his work through. Where are the disciples among the present generation of students agitating in the trade unions way hurling defiance impudently at authority, disobeying teachers or undoing them with threats or thrusts? Above all, how to catch the atmosphere that meant so much for the success of your education?

My rejoinder – first, to the intellectual, 'Pray, have you calculated how many chimera are now actual realities as things of our everyday use, how many Utopias have been worked down into the world of our material living by the powerful constructive genius of men and patient experiments of science in even our life-time? Why not try a little experimentation on human material so full of promise and potentiality, elasticity and metamorphosis, especially when you find and feel it, you are well nigh at the end your armoury of deadly weapons no more terrorises, your bellicose threats hold no people back, your international manipulations turn back on you with frowning faces. Your physical maneuverings are losing acuteness, your mental meanderings are halted before the sandbank of heading deltas in the dwindling flow. But why be disheartened? Hit and head on. Beyond is the vast expanse of the bright sea - the sea of the salts of the earth, with bottoms of pearly bed and treasures spread. To the sympathetic dubious minds my submission - 'why worry so? Do you suppose I want to change everything overnight, or is that possible? How can you supplant all these thousands and thousands of schools? Or, will all the students numbered in millions crowd our schools as soon as they come into existence? And am I to sit sombre and satisfied throwing the vast lots of them upon their fate? None of them.

Reorganizing Education

The present confrontation has come to stay and willy nilly, we have to admire the truth, and I am not discouraged. Give me one or two half-days work in a week in these schools, free from its iron-clad discipline and tight routine business. There, the boys will mix freely, intimately and in a homely way with their preceptors and listen to talks, descriptions and elaborations on the life of India in the Vedic times. They will listen to hymns and prayers recited and must be encouraged to recite themselves. Attempts should be made to provide them with interesting books on the subject with faithful illustration. This I am sure will amply serve our purpose during this spade-work period. What I should insist on is a change of spirit in the mode of work, ideological guidance in favour of the new aim and vision we seek to bring in, and the teachers be inspired to work sincerely and dedicatedly for the purpose. This is, of course, not dispensing with the need of independent schools exclusively dedicated to our ideals. But finance comes to be the hardest and the first hurdle to take in the beginning.

Preceptors to take charge

Our industrial magnates with religious bend have studdded the country with shrines and images maintained at heavy costs. They can be induced to maintain some schools of our ideal on these premises. Some of our duties in famous places of pilgrimage have fabulous income. If properly impressed, these, the management I mean, can divert a portion likewise. But my best faith is in the schools set up with popular efforts - endowments, donations and subscription and gifts volunteered by the people. But everywhere the indispensable and inflexible condition should be to leave the whole show - organisation, management, administration, expansion – entirely into the hands of the preceptors, I mean our present day surrogates of them, the teachers with no right of the financers to interfere beyond advisory suggestions if felt needed. The preceptors in the period of our limited initial work at the starting, I am sure will not be lacking; for I verily believe that India can never be so impoverished as to be depleted of their race in any time of history. With growth in number of schools, I envisage universities coming into existence with affiliating and teaching departments. Here the future generation of preceptors will be turned out, taught, disciplined and trained entirely in the atmosphere and way of life of Vedic times. The affiliating department will not only supervise and correct but disseminate ideals by means of itinerary functions, ceremonials, exhibitions, conferences and congregations, gearing its machinery to work of propaganda and propagation. Researches for improvement and development must also be carried on, one of the most important being to find ways and instruments to break down the walls existing between the state accepted schools of ours, without, of course, deviating in the least from our ideal and goal.

What I conceive to be our goal of perfected achievement is an efflorescence of our institutions now working on modern living to burst into blossoms on its stems, fed and flourishing with the sap and sustenance from Indian roots. Many of our state functions, prefaced now-a-days with featuring of events on Vedic models - like chant of Vedas, and performance of rites reminiscent of Vedic times, evidently betray our affection and admiration for life in ancient India. If these be not political masquerading, the state may well be approached for aids to our work. The Central Government can with full justice take up responsibility to look into its financial side, of course, under conditions of non-interference. The secularism should be no bar. Secularism correctly understood is simply with-holding exercise of state authority in favour of one religion in preference to another. No state can be opposed to improvement in the quality of its citizenship or excellence of character of its individual subjects. The rival claims of other apparently similar bodies -- for each social, political or religious groups to have schools founded and funded by it to doctrinate pupils in its own creed and mould life on its way of thinking will not be justified. For, we strive for liberating education for the nation and the world. In fact, we aspire, and hopefully trust, this 'mankind education' will soon come to occupy the place of our national system of education.

In conclusion we must always bear in mind that social life is a tone and imitation - ninety-five per cent guided by the light and complying with the trend. The five per cent that is individualistic - the galaxy of path-finder seers of new vision, leaders of new spirit in arts and culture, where our drooping life is revitalised and new advance boldly carried, should be left alone to ply their serd time and work unhampered and with the fullest facilities, the ninety-five is to manage the show and maintain the social goal by themselves. If the propaganda and propagation machinery is kept working on the top gears to supply warmth and inducement, there is no fear of our going astray.

Politics of the hallmark of the West now rules the day. It has the largest clientele in the country, for the business pays - at what cost who cares! Favours are not lacking, for the leader must have votes not on merit but with strong barricades of organization. Devotion or earnest work count for nothing if undertaken for general good and not advancing narrow party interest. As a result we have second and third rate men to control the life of the people and shape the destiny of the nation. They are of that diehard race who brought democracy into disrepute and threw the inspiring dreams of a robust new social order into the mud. Ruffled by the man slaughter, social dislocation and aftermath of miseries of people accompanying two global wars occuring in one life time, they have raised the new cry of 'welfare state' to disarm popular discontent and suspicious of revolt. What is at their heart is not general welfare but the loaves and fishes of office and underhand gains of managerial opportunity. Have they put their hands on any radical work for public good or redress social amusementation? They cannot and will not. They have plans and programmes for a future that will never come and they shed oceans of tears over difficulties, tying their hands down. The rainbow bubble must be pricked. The masquerade forced to a termination, the actors being shown in their true colours. The grip of governmental interference is tightening faster than ever before, and people are reduced to a new state of thraldom, with handicaps stealthily spreading. Citizens must be allowed maximum freedom to realise their responsibility and play their proper role in the set up. That is the way to a true welfare state. What is done is a part of the dark design to keep people out of the harm's way. The deceptive crooks must be eliminated and be always kept at arm's length, if ever we seek to implement a welfare state and do the people good and ensure even-handed justice, advancing all to prosperity. But remember, that too is only a half way home, where, if we linger long resting or guesting, the fruits of our achievement are sure to fall off like leaves in a winter night. For, social inspiration and sincere work have never any durable life, we must enter the God's life-citadel where everything is permanent and eternal.

The Three Pillars

Three things are considered as essential prerequisites, indispensable concomitants to the success of our process, the three corner-stones on which our projected edifice is to stand firm. The first and, no doubt, the foremost - the very matrix to support the structure, is a free and adequate supply of preceptors to spread like a network all over the country, not, however, letting quality suffer for the need of quantity. They are indeed the soul of the education - inspiration, achievement and future advancement resting on their ability and personality and drive. They are not only to keep schools but with people giving their dealings and conduct a new direction, stimulating ideals and for a new social trend. His personality will be here the asset as nothing else can be. The most important business here is to maintain them in independence, in the dignity of high social respect.

The next thing - curious it may seem but indispensable, in the orientation–is the cultivation, as a social habit, of a serious and sincere faith in the existence of God as the ultimate will, determining the course of life and worldly events and that transgression never can go scot-free, discredits or distress dogging the steps or as the Hindu belief goes, a most condemned after birth existence of torture, social ignominy and privation and being the rewards of an obeying life. The conviction has to be rooted in all minds that an absolute just supreme power controls things and man is not free to do as he pleases with his intellect's guide and is seriously answerable for cruelties, inflicted injuries and miseries and destructive works done to creation or the world. Our desperate political purposes and dark narrow self-seeking designs need a check and this is the only way. To try to prove or disprove the existence of God, at this hour of the day, is like carrying coal to Newcastle. But as the serious and acutely analytical Aldous Huxley says, 'How can you doubt when the experience and feelings of man, far apart in time and countries, so correspond. We blunder - God is not a matter of material intellectual reasoning but of supramental perception.'

Our Upanishads say: He, who says, 'I know', is ignorant, and he, who says, 'know not but have felt flitting touches' is the real knower, and warns that to remain satisfied in ignorance of the spirit is the ruin of a life. Our religious books say, 'God alone knows what he is.' We ought to be guided by the light passed on to us by saints or sages through long ages who have declared, in no equivocal terms, their knowledge and vision of God. Our *Gita* gives an excellent hint as a proof of God's existence. God says - 'whenever you see in a personality a force vast and transcending, defying the barricade of difficulties of time and social trend, know me manifesting there.' Need we belittle or thrust aside the truth except for flattering our renegade arrogance. The record of our century long living in Godlessness with science as guide and accomplice is no happy or inspiring one or anything we can look back upon with pride. Why then, this bravado? God in his infinite mercy, sincerity, knowledge and power takes the world to prosperity and perfection, evenly dealt out helps us get free from the heavy brassnels of narrow self-seeking and work in harmony with this will.

The third thing is reverence. It is no foolish worship of the traditional respect nor any suspension of one's independent judgement or rejection of felt-truth, nor even silencing a robust protest felt needed. It is simply a mental decorum to be practised for listening with grace and propriety of manners to what others say or may have to say. Opinions put forward different aspects of truth revealed to different minds helping us to compare, combine, eliminate and arrive at the broadest conclusion with respect to that truth on which alone society can thrive. To be divorced from reverence is to be a hollow tree with all prospects of pith and growth blighted. Let knowledge grow from more, to more says the same poet of high human wisdom. The arduous effort to arrive at the largest extent of truth is synonymous with reverence. Can we hope to keep the social fabric strong by doing away with reverence? Let more of reverence in us dwell.

In Conclusion

The crisis facing us is not amenable to any local treatment or piecemeal solution. For verily we live in one world - the impact of one part powerfully reacting in another. But the tragedy of thing - it is one world on its physical aspect only - contact of people, purchase of necessities and luxuries, commercial combines, friendly profit-sharing, etc. On the mental side, the world is parted, parcelled, walled round into bits, each pulling in its own way. The tangled ramifications and crooked roots underground pushing deep and fast clinging to several narrow self-interests or time-serving national opportunities. Governments press on entrenched move than ever before, sitting secure on their armoury of deadly weapons, and the broad shoulders of jingoist patriotism will laugh down any proposal of sober counsel for restraint or change of motives as derogatory to national prestige. They can only be brought to their knees by threats of being overthrown. Happily for us, we now here, in every country, two trends - the jingoist and the earnest pacifist – both running in juxtaposition and interpenetration, vying for supremacy of control - the result of revulsions born of the shocks of ruinous wars. India with her peace-loving ways and will to universal good must do all she can to swell the trend for peace, with heart within and God over head. We do not know the wonders God's mercy can work. The West with its ardour for progress and habit of experimenting with new things and a life view all dynamic, if once convinced of the value of renuniciation, detachment, Godly living as conveying richer returns, taste of life and a new thrill of the joys of existence will surely take kindly to the new mode and a time of new hopes and bright promises will dawn on earth. Will that not be a proud day for India, if she be acknowledged in the lead?

India's approach to life is peculiar but very significant, conceived in terms of fervent dynamism held fast within the bounds of a static framework-life a baffling mystery, an unending curiosity, a centre of fascinating interest and inexhaustible experience in which growth and change, movement and stablisation mingle in an inscrutable oneness of process. The child is not the same as he is in adolescence, in youth, in manhood, but the identity never comes under a challenge or is never lost. It has satisfied the spiritual hunger of the easy believing men of old, it is satisfying the intellectual demands of our present critically analytic age. The place of action is recognised and given its value as aids to unfolding and enriching life but a steadfast, meditative repose in the recess of being as a link with the absolute remains the goal - the final achievement of life's purpose. There, he is the being - the reflection of the eternal changeless being. Here, we are 'becoming' through change, manifestation and growth on the drive of action.

Our concept of life is that of something with layer on layer of coats giving it a solid tight appearance. As the coats are lifted, newer and newer shapes are revealed till in the end we are overwhelmed by a strong transformation of the scene. The surface coat is the thickest and the hardest, held tight by the pressure, so to say, of the world around and most difficult to remove. This is also the battle ground of lures, attractions, worldly ambitions preying on our minds and this, we call life, as we ordinarily know it. Here, we gather knowledge and experience and organise our personality to face the battle of life, the world and the divine. This coat, once lifted, as we move inwards and towards the center, the coats grow thinner and more and more transparent, admitting the light from central core, and progress becomes easy and sure. In each layer, we enter different worlds of different perception and meanings grow fuller, and clearer relations are revealed in subtler, nearer and deeper closeness with creation. Knowledge becomes broader, more penetrative, enriched with finer shades and brighter fringes - the very personality organisation getting looser, softer and more malleable till on re-coming into the centre, crude physical elements with all their control and cohesion and influence gone. Life seems to be an airy form melting and flowing in oneness with current of creation with an expansion of life and delight we never felt in encagement of the gross form of what is currently called life. The center, the true essence of our being is all light and all calm steeped in unthinkable emanation of beauty and love. We are dissolved and absorbed and liberated from fetters of narrow individual existence. It is here, our indwelling god (the soul divine expanded) and the God of the universe, the supreme existence merged in oneness, we realise the truth and ultimate reality of creation and the meaning of individual existence - God spirit with a distinctive name mark of separation. It is particularly to be noted that after the experience our physical elements undergo a complete change wholly divinised and no longer preyed upon by mundane promptings or worldly bindings, it be challenged, life nestled in this sanctum and cradled in the swing of this life activity only is to furnish the army to reclaim our world out of its present sad state of decay and decadence. Nay! it is no *statusquo* maintaining the order of the world in constrained peace and customary progress. It is an uprise - a prosperity, a richness, a social efflorescence, we can never imagine with thoughts crippled into the limitation of the present, memory burdened with the darkness of the past. Renunication is now enjoyment - a personal share foregone to delight another in difficulty, love unstinted and freed, a pouring like God's mercy resuscitating and brightening every dropping reality and relation to God's purity and tranquillity, a balm of loving life, society, creation and reigning supreme, and we are ushered into a world, smiling like a summer day. Social activity is worship and worship is now the business of life. We can hardly imagine even the vitality such living will release. Verily, those will be the days making countries overflow with milk and honey.

With a bank of preceptors worthy of their mission fully grounded in the knowledge and practice of thin truth of life and reality of creation, with numberless disciples disciplined, taught and trained to perfection, carrying to every nook and corner of the country this message and familiarising all with glorious vision each life latently carries, all working in one spirit, heart and soul to bring down to parallel this world of our living of God's in glory as a handiwork of his own. Our Vedic ancestors hit upon a way of life and a social organisation still the world wonders and we accept with only half faith - a life in God and of God's. The vedic education was the product of this life and as much as the inspirer of it. If we can rouse ourselves by the education and live true to the ideas and ideals it presents, the world will have an example to follow. Here is perfection, here is liberation, work and detachment going hand in hand, here is the rest of the turmoil of worldly life and individual living. It is afar way forms of politics and a surface-soaked social reforms. Jesus said, amidst and profanations of the synagoure, ' I have come to fulfill and not to destroy! That is god's voice. The splendid civilization so rich, so inspiring so unflinchingly devoted to search of truth, is not to be destroyed but fulfilled. India holds the light to guide along the slippery and deceptive path. We do not know what God can do when he so wills.

"Man is the measure of all things", said Aristotle styled 'Master of those who know' infinitude to his massive intellect and rare wisdom, never suspecting this summit truth of social living could ever be assailed, and satisfied perhaps, being able to provide mankind with such a permanent measuring rod. Worn thin and short by the wear and tear of time, the rod is rejected and replaced by one put into the hands of his ignoranous voterus by God Mammoth, and with us money has become the measure, and we jubilate, being able to tumble Pallas down from her seat of importance and glory. But like God, truth is not mocked and we are paying the high price for our wanton mocking. The West believes in machine in its organised efficiency and unfailing output. But it has no heart; crushes life out of existence in its triumphant march, India believes in the native Godness of man, in his stupendous possibility of glorious becoming. Put him on his greatness and on the high truth of his existence and the world will go and grow gloriously. Thou art God's Jery self, says the Veda. 'Man Thou art greater than the earth, the space between earth and heaven than heaven itself (its joys being limited to time) than even all the worlds of cosmic creation taken together? Not possession, nor power, nor the noise you make in the world but in the manifested glory of your native greatness that you are fulfilled' say, the Upanishads. Sons of India, you were taught the prayer of eternal India - speed us on from the momentary to the permanent, from darkness to light, from death (of frivolous living) to life eternal. On thou the supreme manifestation, possess me and be mine who in his sense with this immense, splendid heritage in his possession would barter away the vast indescribable dower for the tinsel glamour of worldly success. In the *Puranas*, there is a story - funny but extremely significant – as showing the love and inertia of a current existence, Vishnu, the sustainer and maintainer of creation once came into the world in the body of a boar to rid creation of a disturbing catastrophe. Mission accomplished, he lived on in the base existence, happy with his boar wife and pig children while the order of creation went topsy. Turning for want of Vishnu's work, at the request of all Gods, Shiva – the God of death as well as of eternal bliss – came down and pricked him with his death dealing trident and ended the funny show. Vishnu laughed and went to take up duties of his office. Let us too be relieved of the lethargy of the boarish existence being pricked by the trident of God, glory and eternal truth of life. Let God live, let love prosper, but life thrive. Let creation be revealed in beauty, light and eternal progress. Let not its heavenly face be scarred by any of our wanton doing. Amen!

Epilogue

Ancient and Modern Indian Education: The Verge

Marmar Mukhopadhyay

Like all other social institutions, education too is guided by a set of principles and practices. This was true in ancient days of 'ancient Indian education'; this is equally true today. Moot questions are: Are the principles of ancient Indian education still valid? Have they changed? Are the practices of ancient Indian education still valid? Have they changed? Has the genuineness of the education system changed over time? By genuineness, I mean the convergence between principles and practices. The intensive research on ancient Indian education (Das 1996, Mookerjee 1969, Keay 1980) clearly reveals close proximity between principles and practices. It walked what it talked. My well considered hypothesis is the ever widening gap between the stated educational principles and practices in modern day education. This lack of genuineness has created either human robots or animals walking on two legs. The author rightly points out towards the social decadence. The core of decadence — individual, group, social, national and international — is due to erosion of higher human values; honesty, integrity, reverence, austerity, discipline, knowledge seeking, etc.

Educational principles, today, do not campaign for corruption, sexual promiscuity and women as object of lust, cowardice, self-seeking, etc. On the contrary, there is an articulated policy and principle of universal values that has stood guarantee to human civilization through the corridors of human history. There is a directive to teach fundamental duties enshrined in Indian Constitution. The problem is in the practices; these have moved miles away from the stated principles.

Let us illustrate the point. *Sa vidya ya vimuktaye* or emancipation has been a stated and cherished goal of education, then, as well as now. When son of Jabala, a prostitute approached Guru Gautam for admission to his class, Guru asked him his *gotra* (caste). The child admitted that he did not know. Guru Gautam asked him to go back, find out his *gotra* from his mother and come back. The boy was back to the Guru after a few days. When he was asked about his *gotra*, without hesitation he told what his mother had told — she served many men to earn her living, so she did not know whose child was he and what was his *gotra*. When all other disciples laughed at him, Guru Gautam walked upto the child, took him in his lap and said - 'I know your *gotra*, you are born in 'Truth' caste. He admitted the child and named him 'Satyakaam'. Thus, emancipation was preached and practised. Today, when education is guaranteed to all as a fundamental right, a child (may or may not be an offspring of a prostitute) without father's name finds Himalayan obstruction to find a place in a school. This verge in the principles and practices have led to people in exalted positions of power to look for their cousins of various origins - family, political, linguistic, geographic affiliations for important positions in total disregard of the capable and competent ones.

Education began at 'Brahmacharyashram'- with the concept of life in Brahma in tune with the Vedic understanding of nature of human beings as divine — *amritasya putra* — child of immortality. This understanding is corroborated by all religions as is evident from interfaith research on education (Mukhopadhyay, 2003). Necessarily, the emphasis was on purity of conduct which is God's own attribute. In 'Brahmacharyashram', disciples (one who practises discipline, compared to a student who studies) practised purity of conduct through out the day in all that they did. Purity of conduct is as cherished a principle today as it was in the past. However, there is an aberration in practice. Educational practices, now, are guided by short term goals and gains. I have not come across anyone during my last forty years in education — teachers, students and parents — who champions impure and bad conduct. Relevant question is what Arjuna asked Sri Krishna:

'Atha kena prayuktouang papan carati purushaha
Anichhannapi varshneya valadivaniyojitaha'
(-Sl.36, Ch.3)

-- impelled by what, men commit sin even involuntarily, as though driven by force?

Sri Krishna's clarification is equally important: it is the insatiable desire driven by *Rajasik* qualities which is the enemy in this case. The studentship that cultivates cognition, that too marginally, does not discipline that desire which disciples were trained in 'Brahmacharyashram'.

Ancient Indian education stood for education in a wide variety of subjects and in specializations. Education invariably cultivated life skills as is evident from the practices in the Gurukula system. Also, each learner had a curriculum according to his/her propensities, and each had to reach the mastery level before they could leave the Gurukula for their parents homes. Arjuna had to pierce the eyeball of the bird to qualify. There is no difference in these principles too. Modern education too stands for specialization on the foundation of broad spectrum general education (secondary education). It champions individualized instruction. It has experimented and professed mastery learning (Benjamin Bloom's contribution). The difference is in practice. The industrial model of classroom based education misconstrued teacher's role. Teacher teaches; the responsibility of learning is left to students. Learning is not ensured. There is an ever widening gap between knowledge creation and knowledge absorption (Mukhopadhyay, 2003) resulting into huge educational loss - less than 13% of those enrolled in standard one qualify as school graduate in India on the face of proven evidence of mastery learning.

There is again a concurrence on principle about the methods of transaction. Both ancient Indian education and modern education championed multi-channel learning (Anzalone 1995, Mukhopadhyay 1995). Hastana Satak contains:

'*Acaryat padamadatte,*
Padam sishya swamedhaya
Padamekam swabrahmachirivvi,
Padam kalakramenahim'

-- one quarter of learning accrues from teacher, another from self learning, a third quarter from the peer group (cooperative learning) and remaining with time (experiential learning). Both ancient and modern education advocates constructivist approach to learning. There is, however, a wide gap in the practice in modern Indian education. In the Gurukula tradition, there was definite provision for and practice of all the four channels as enunciated by the author as well as his predecessors. Modern Indian education has restricted itself to behaviourism and instructivist processes of learning that is teacher centered. It focusses on teaching not necessarily on learning.

The center of gravity of this widening gap in modern education between principles and practices is in teacher behaviour. In ancient Indian education, Guru's life was not only an open book, it was also the most important live-book where the disciples learnt their ways of life. Guru insisted on doing what he did rather than what he preached. Each disciple was thoroughly exposed to Guru's learning habits and commitment, purity of conduct, family life, reverence for guests, etc. And, his/her overarching affiliation to the divine as the guiding light. Compared to that, a large majority of modern day teachers trade in education. Exceptions apart, large number of teachers teach without preparedness, assess students without adequate care, take to private tuition and favour 'private students'. Unlike the ancient Indian education, students are exposed to indiscipline, greed, poor scholarship, lack of genuineness in learning habits, and poor conduct of the teachers. The gap between preaching and practice in education is too wide and visible to students. They are immediately exposed to disvalues. Values can rarely be taught like any other subject; values are lived and hence inculcated through demonstration by teachers and elders, and imitation by students. The decadence of our times is because of this value crisis; because of poor demonstration of values as lived by teachers and elders in the society.

Unlike the ancient Indian education modern Indian education is provided by five million teachers. It is no more possible to induct only those as preceptors into education who are mentally and spiritually equipped for the role. Challenge is much larger with ever expanding base of education due to increasing democratization.

There is a definite case to revisit education, particularly in terms of practices. Vedantic tradition then, and International Commission on Education for 21st Century (UNESCO, 1996) now proclaims education for nurturing physical, mental, intellectual and spiritual planes. Yoga, discourses, peer group interaction, learning to live together, spiritual practices in Gurukula ensured holistic all round development. Modern Indian education lost its way in creating clerks (ghost of Lord Macaulay is still haunting) out of young minds. It nurtured only the intellectual plane of living, that too at lower order cognition far below the level of creativity. Physical education concentrated on body building without building the inner strength. Emotional development that houses the human values has been given a go bye; spiritual education, even education about religions are untouchable.

It would be evident from the above analysis that the principles of education has stood the test of time. Modern education has lost on practice due to the domination of *Rajasik* qualities - insatiable desire for material gains distancing the concept of human being from the divine (the renunciate) into the proximity of animality (the self-seeking). Argument is not for closing down schools and colleges and start Gurukulas. Argument is for a shift in practice to bring it closer to principles. It does not require extra financial resources; it needs a change of thc mind set - putting higher priority to *Swattik* qualities over *Rajasik* ones.

The nostalgic reaction is to bring back ancient education lock stock and barrel to modern India. Cynical reaction is to reject out right the ancient educational system. More rational approach is to examine what are those universal principles that were practised in ancient Indian education and can still be practised. Just as an example, there are about 5000 private schools with about 40,000 teachers. they are well paid compared to teachers even a decade ago. They have a small family to look after. If each teacher houses one socially and economically deprived child at his/her home and educates in his/her quality school, 40,000 children can afford private school education. And, teachers, life becomes their book of learning. This transparency would significantly improve the personal and professional conduct of teachers which no teacher training programme will ever be able to inculcate. There can be many such innovations in modern Indian education that can be inspired by ancient Indian education.

References

Anzalone, S., The case for multi-channel learning, in Anzalone, S. (ed). *Multi-channel Learning: Connecting All to Education*, Washington D.C.: EDC, 1995.

Das, Santosh K. *Education System of the Ancient Indian Hindus*, New Delhi: Gyan, 1986

Keay, F. E. *Ancient Indian Education*, New Delhi: COSMO, 1980.

Mukherjee, R.K., *Ancient Indian Education*, Allahabad: Motilal Banarasidas, 1969

Mukhopadhyay, Marmar, Multi-channel Learning: Case of National Open School, in Anzalone, S. (ed), *Multi-channel Learning: Connecting All to Education*, Washington, EDC, 1995.

Mukhopadhyay, Marmar (ed), *Education for a Global Society: Interfaith Dimensions*, New Delhi: Shipra, 2003.

Mukhopadhyay, Marmar (ed), *Educational Technology: Knowledge Assessment*, New Delhi; In Press, 2003

UNESCO, *Learning: The Treasure Within*, Paris: UNESCO, 1996.